Noah

pictures by Ken Munowitz

text by Charles L. Mee, Jr.

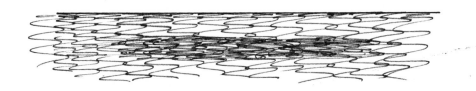

Harper & Row, Publishers

New York, Hagerstown, San Francisco, London

For Milton and Norma — K.M.

For Deborah and Karen — C.M.

NOAH
Text copyright © 1978 by Charles L. Mee, Jr.
Illustrations copyright © 1978 by Ken Munowitz

FIRST EDITION

Library of Congress Cataloging in Publication Data
Munowitz, Ken.
    Noah.

    SUMMARY: Retells the story of how Noah and his family
built the ark and saved the animals from the Great Flood.
    1. Noah's ark — Juvenile literature.   [1. Noah's ark.
2. Bible stories — O.T.]   I. Mee, Charles L.   II. Title.
BS658.M78 1978   222'1'09505   77-11839
ISBN 0-06-024183-7
ISBN 0-06-024184-5 lib. bdg.

The Bible is a book of stories
thousands of years old.
This is one of the stories of the Bible.

The world was full
of shouting and fighting and killing,
and God said, "This must stop."
But it did not.
So God said, "I will destroy every living thing
that I created on the earth,
all men and women and animals.
I will make it rain and rain
until I flood the whole world."

But Noah and his wife were good.

So God told them to take their family,

and build a huge boat, an ark,

three stories high, with many rooms,

and fill it with two of every kind of animal,

male and female,

all those that walked or crawled or flew.

For soon, God said, it would rain.

"I will build the ark," said Noah,

"with the help of my three sons."

Noah and his family
gathered all the animals.

And, soon, it began to rain.

The rain covered the highest mountains,

and lifted up the ark above the land.

The rain drowned all who were on the land below.

The animals stayed inside the ark,

two by two,

And Noah and his family cared for them,

And they waited for the rain to stop.

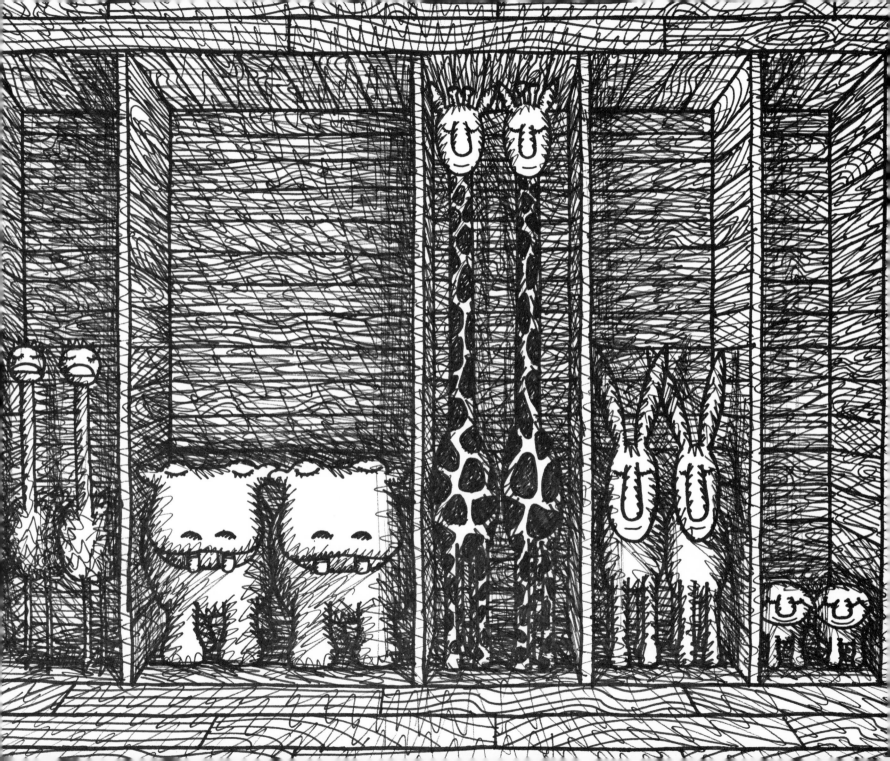

After forty days and forty nights,
the rain did stop.
And Noah's ark rested
on the very top
of a mountain named Ararat.

Noah sent out a dove to look for land.

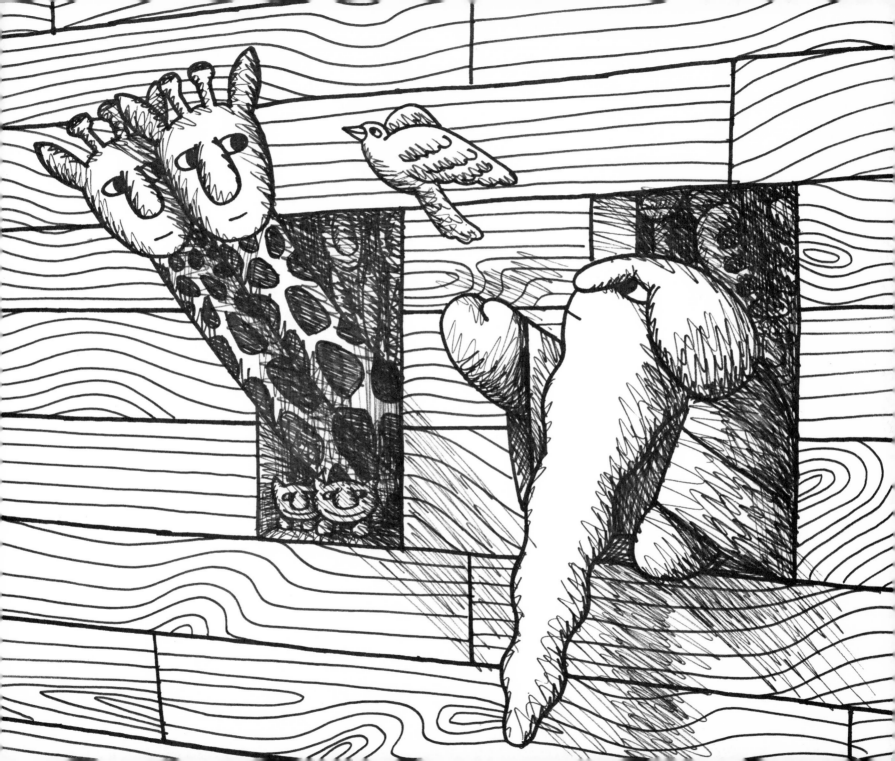

The dove found land,

and brought back an olive branch

to prove it.

Soon the water got lower,

and the ark was left on dry land.

Then God sent a rainbow,
the first that was ever seen.
He promised that He would never
flood the earth again.

And Noah and his family, and all the animals,

left the ark and filled the earth once more

with the miracle of life.